First Facts™

Learning about Money

Saving Money

by Mary Firestone

Consultant:
Sharon M. Danes, PhD
Professor and Family Economist
University of Minnesota

Capstone
press

Mankato, Minnesota

First Facts is published by Capstone Press
151 Good Counsel Drive, P.O. Box 669, Mankato, Minnesota 56002
www.capstonepress.com

Library of Congress Cataloging-in-Publication Data
Firestone, Mary.
    Saving money / by Mary Firestone.
    p. cm.—(First facts. Learning about money)
    Includes bibliographical references and index.
    ISBN-13: 978-0-7368-2640-2 (hardcover)
    ISBN-10: 0-7368-2640-8 (hardcover)
    1. Finance, Personal—Juvenile literature. 2. Saving and investment—Juvenile literature.
I. Title. II. Series.
HG179.F533 2005
332.024′0083—dc22   2004000393

Summary: Uses text and photographs to discuss how and why to save money.

Editorial Credits
Heather Adamson, editor; Jennifer Bergstrom, designer; Scott Thoms, photo researcher;
    Eric Kudalis, product planning editor

Photo Credits
Capstone Press/Gary Sundermeyer, cover (foreground), 5, 6–7, 8 (foreground), 9, 10–11, 13, 14, 15,
    16–17, 19 (foreground)
Citizen Information Center, City of Lincoln, 20
Comstock Inc., 1 (all)
EyeWire Images, back cover
Image Club, 8 (background)
Image Ideas, 19 (background)
PhotoDisc Inc., cover

022010
5678R

Table of Contents

Saving Money

Dora has $5. She puts $2 in her "save" jar. She is saving for a scooter. She **needs** $1 to buy milk at school. Dora also **wants** to spend $1 at the arcade. She puts the last dollar in her "share" jar to give to others. Saving money helps you buy things you need and want.

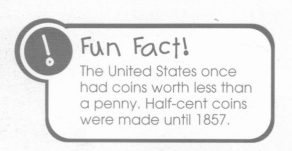

Fun Fact!

The United States once had coins worth less than a penny. Half-cent coins were made until 1857.

Earnings	
birthday	$3
allowance	$2
Total Earnings	$5

Total Earnings	$5
- Savings	$2
Money to spend	$3

Costs	
milk	$1
Sharing	$1
Arcade	$1
Total costs	$3

How to Save

Putting money aside before you spend it helps you save. **Earnings** are money that you are paid or given. Costs are money you spend buying things. To save money, your earnings must be more than costs. Dora spends only part of her earnings so she can save the rest.

Saving for Later

You can save money to use later. You could use it for yourself or use it for others. Dora shares some money she saves with others who need it.

8

Saving lets you buy more costly items without **borrowing** from others. Dora saves a little of her money each week. In time, she will save enough for a scooter.

Savings Add Up

Small amounts of money add up over time. If you put $2 in a jar each week, you will have $8 at the end of the month. After saving for a year, you would have more than $100.

pend

Share

Save

Keeping Savings at Home

Saving money at home is easy. You can put the money you save in a jar or piggy bank. As you add money, you can watch the jar fill with your savings.

Fun Fact!

Money once was kept in jars made from pygg clay. Artists started shaping the jars like pigs. These were called piggy banks.

13

Keeping Savings at a Bank

You can keep your savings at a bank. Banks pay **interest**. Interest is a little bit of money the bank gives you for keeping money at their bank.

Dora writes what she brings to the bank in a **passbook**. When she wants to spend her money, the bank will give it back with interest.

Other Ways to Save

Jars and banks are not the only ways to save money. Savings bonds earn money when you keep them for many years. Bonds can help you save for college or things you need in the future.

Fun Fact!

In 1941, a $50 savings bond cost $37.50. That bond would be worth $181.18 in 2005.

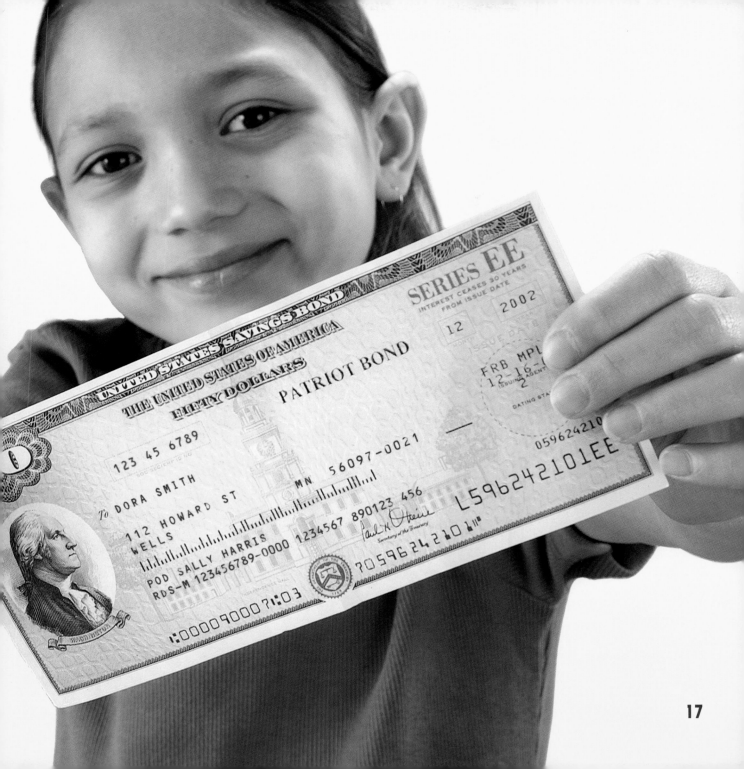

SERIES EE
INTEREST CEASES 30 YEARS
FROM ISSUE DATE

12   2002

THE UNITED STATES OF AMERICA
UNITED STATES SAVINGS BOND
FIFTY DOLLARS   PATRIOT BOND

123 45 6789

To DORA SMITH
112 HOWARD ST   MN   56097-0021
WELLS
POD SALLY HARRIS
RDS-M 123456789-0000 1234567 890123 456

FRB MPL
12-16-0

059624210

L596242101EE

70 596 24 2101

Paul H. O'Neill
Secretary of the Treasury

I:000090007I:03

Saving Is Smart

Saving money is a good choice. Saving money now will help you buy things you will need and want later. Dora saved enough to buy her own scooter. Saving money helps you plan for the future.

Jim Hruska saved pennies for 30 years. He collected more than 30,000 pennies. In 2000, he donated his pennies. He helped pay for a statue of Abraham Lincoln in Lincoln, Nebraska.

Hands On: Make Money Jars

You can make money jars to sort your money. You can use your jars to help you spend, save, and share.

What You Need

markers
paper
3 clean jars
tape
coins

What You Do

1. Use markers and paper to make labels for your jars. Write a label saying, "Save," a label saying, "Share," and a label saying, "Spend."
2. Tape a label to each jar.
3. You can make pictures for reminders of how the money in each jar will be used. Tape these to the outside of your jars.
4. Decide how many coins to put in each jar. Put the coins in the jar and keep adding coins every week. Follow the labels on your jars. Then you will have money to spend, to share, and to save.

Glossary

borrow (BOR-oh)—to use something that belongs to someone else; money that is borrowed must be returned.

earnings (URN-ings)—money received for working or sometimes as a gift; children's earnings often come from allowances or gifts.

interest (IN-trist)—an extra bit of money banks pay as a reward for saving

need (NEED)—to require something; you need food, shelter, and clothes to stay alive.

passbook (PASS-buk)—a notebook that banks give people to help them keep track of the money they save

want (WONT)—to feel you would like to have something; you may want a new bike or a snack.

Read More

Mayr, Diane. *The Everything Kids' Money Book: From Saving to Spending to Investing—Learn All about Money!* Holbrook, Mass.: Adams Media Corp., 2000.

Rosinsky, Natalie M. *Saving Money.* Let's See Library. Economics. Minneapolis: Compass Point Books, 2004.

Internet Sites

FactHound offers a safe, fun way to find Internet sites related to this book. All of the sites on FactHound have been researched by our staff.

Here's how:
1. Visit *www.facthound.com*
2. Type in this special code **0736826408** for age-appropriate sites. Or enter a search word related to this book for a more general search.
3. Click on the **Fetch It** button.

FactHound will fetch the best sites for you!

Index